ROCKS, MINERALS, AND RESOURCES

World of Water

Essential to life

Rona Arato

Crabtree Publishing Company
www.crabtreebooks.com

Crabtree Publishing Company
www.crabtreebooks.com

Coordinating editor: Ellen Rodger

Production coordinator: Rosie Gowsell

Design: Samara Parent

Editors: Amanda Bishop, Ellen Rodger

Proofreader and Indexer: Adrianna Morganelli

Production assistant: Samara Parent

Scanning technician: Arlene Arch-Wilson

Art director: Rob MacGregor

Photo research: Allison Napier

Consultant: Dr. Richard Cheel, Professor of Earth Sciences, Brock University

Photographs: Paul Almos/CORBIS: p. 24; AP/ Wide World Photos: p. 6, p. 19 (top left), p. 21 (top right), p. 22, p. 27 (bottom), p. 31 (bottom right); Archive/ Photo Researchers, Inc: p. 13; John Beatty/ Photo Researchers, Inc: p. 9; George Bernard/ Photo Researchers, Inc: p. 12; Gregory G. Dimijian/ Photo Researchers, Inc: p. 20 (left); Dennis Flaherty/ Photo Researchers, Inc: p. 18; Lowell Georgia/ Photo Researchers, Inc: p. 30; Gavin Hellier/ Getty Images: p. 1; Ed Kashi/ CORBIS: p. 16 (top right), p. 23; Noel R. Kemp/ Photo Researchers, Inc: p. 28; Wayne Lawler/ Photo Researchers, Inc: p. 21 (bottom); Ken Lax/ Photo Researchers, Inc: p. 11 (top left); Lester Lefkowitz/ CORBIS: p. 26; Danny Lehman/ CORBIS: p.19 (bottom); Guy Mansfield/ Panos Pictures: p. 20 (bottom right); David Muench/ CORBIS: p. 29 (bottom right); NASA/ Photo Researchers, Inc: p. 17 (top left); Samara Parent: p. 27 (top right); Carl Purcell/ Photo Researchers, Inc: p. 7 (top left); Roger Ressmeyer/ CORBIS: p. 29 (top left); Karen Robinson/ Panos Pictures: P. 31 (top left); Joseph Sohm; Visions of America/ CORBIS: p. 8 (bottom); Paul A. Souders/ CORBIS: p. 25; Jim Steinberg/ Photo Researchers, Inc: p. 17 (bottom right); David Turnley/ CORBIS: p. 16 (bottom); Kennan Ward/ CORBIS: p. 7 (bottom right); K. M. Westerman/ CORBIS: p. 15; Ian Yates; Eye Ubiquitous/ CORBIS: p. 8 (top right).

Illustrations: Roman Goforth: p. 3, pp. 4-5; Dan Pressman: p. 10

Cover: Water is used to irrigate fields in the United States.

Title page: The melting of the glacier supplies this river and the people, plants, and animals, who depend on it, with freshwater.

Crabtree Publishing Company

www.crabtreebooks.com   1-800-387-7650

Cataloging-in-Publication Data

Arato, Rona.
    World of water / written by Rona Arato.
        p. cm. -- (Rocks, minerals, and resources)
    Includes index.
    ISBN 0-7787-1416-0 (rlb) -- ISBN 0-7787-1448-9 (pb)
    1. Water--Juvenile literature. I. Title. II. Series.
    GB662.3.A73 2005
    551.48--dc22
                                                2004012812
                                                LC

Published in the United States
PMB 16A
350 Fifth Ave.
Suite 3308
New York, NY
10118

Published in Canada
616 Welland Ave.,
St. Catharines,
Ontario, Canada
L2M 5V6

Published in the United Kingdom
73 Lime Walk
Headington
Oxford
0X3 7AD
United Kingdom

Published in Australia
386 Mt. Alexander Rd.,
Ascot Vale (Melbourne)
V1C 3032

Contents

Testing 1-2-3!

The lake stretched before them, a blue mirror reflecting a cloudless sky. The class was collecting water samples from the lake. Each child, now a detective, filled a jar with water. Back at school they would test their samples. Their teacher had said that the clearest lakes were often dead. Was this a healthy lake, teeming with life? Had pollution damaged it? They would use science to find out for sure.

The blue planet

Living things cannot exist without water. We use water to drink, wash, and cook. Waterpower generates electricity to give us light and heat, and to run machines such as refrigerators and computers. People travel on waterways, such as lakes, rivers, and oceans. Without water there would be no trees, flowers, fruits, or vegetables. Water gives life and makes Earth different from every planet in our **solar system**.

5

What is water?

Photos from space show the Earth covered with water and dotted with chunks of land. Water – tons and tons of it – makes up a life-giving network of oceans, rivers, lakes, and streams.

What is water made from?

Water is colorless, **transparent**, tasteless, and odorless. Water is a **chemical** compound, or mixture, made of two **elements** – hydrogen and oxygen.

The chemistry of water

The chemical symbol for water is H_2O. A water **molecule** is made up of two atoms, or very small parts, of hydrogen (H) and one atom of oxygen (O). Water contains many other materials because wherever it goes, it picks up substances such as **minerals** in the ground or on the surface.

The universal solvent

Scientists call water the universal **solvent** because water dissolves, or breaks down, more things than any other liquid. Many things dissolve or disappear in water because water molecules are small and move easily around other molecules. When a substance dissolves in water, the water takes on its character. For example, dissolving sugar in water makes the water sweet. Dissolving salt in water makes the water salty.

About 97 percent of the Earth's water is in its oceans.

Two types of water

There are two types of water, saltwater and freshwater. Most of the Earth is covered with saltwater. Saltwater is found in all the oceans. Salt is a mineral called sodium chloride, made up of the elements sodium and chlorine. The sodium comes from rain wearing away at rocks and dissolving the sodium, which is carried to the oceans in water. Chlorine comes from the eruption of underwater volcanoes. When these two elements meet in water, saltwater forms. Freshwater also contains tiny amounts of salt and other minerals. Living things on land, including humans, drink freshwater. Freshwater is found in some rivers, lakes, and streams.

(above) The Dead Sea is so salty that bathers float on top of the water instead of sinking.

Salinity

Salinity is the amount of salt dissolved in a liquid. Ocean water is too salty to drink. There is so much salt in the world's oceans, that if it was all removed it would cover the Earth in a layer 500 feet (152 meters) thick. Ocean water is less salty at the equator, where heavy rain adds more freshwater to the oceans. Ocean water near coastal areas is also less salty because of freshwater runoff from rivers and streams.

Rock formations and salt deposits surround ancient Mono Lake in California. The lake's salt content is two and a half times that of the Pacific Ocean.

Liquid, solid, gas

Water is found in three states: liquid, solid, and gas. The liquid state is water, the solid state is ice, and the gas state is vapor.

Water molecules

Water molecules are always moving. When they heat up, they move faster and closer together. That is why hot water boils. As they move even faster, they move farther apart and become water vapor, which rises into the air. Cold water molecules move slowly, become farther from each other, and form ice or a solid surface.

(above) Geothermal energy is heat from inside the Earth. The heat can rise through cracks in the surface and heat bodies of water, such as these thermal baths in Iceland.

(below) Glaciers, such as this one in Argentina, are large rivers of flowing ice. Chunks of solid ice break off and eventually melt into rivers or oceans.

Float or sink?

Water has important properties, or attributes, that determine how it is used and in what state. Water pressure is the property measured by the weight of water above an object. The deeper the object is submerged, the more the water above it weighs. Buoyancy is the property that makes an object weigh less in water than in air. Buoyancy happens because water exerts an upward force on a submerged object. This is why objects float in water. Salt increases buoyancy in water, making it easier for people to swim in saltwater than in freshwater.

Density and freezing

Density is the bulk or compactness of water. Water is the only substance that is less dense in solid form than in liquid form. Water is most dense at 39.2° Fahrenheit (4° Celsius), just before freezing. As water gets colder, molecules move farther apart and the water becomes lighter. By the time it becomes ice at 32° Fahrenheit (0° Celsius), the molecules have moved apart and become less dense. This is why ice floats.

Calculating sea level

Sea level refers to the level of the surface of the sea, or any surface that is on the same level with the sea. Sea level is used as the base to measure land surfaces or ocean depths. At sea level, water freezes at 32° Fahrenheit (0° Celsius) and boils at 212° Fahrenheit (100° Celsius). The boiling temperature drops at higher altitudes. For example, at a height of 14,000 feet (4,267 meters) water boils at 186.4° Fahrenheit (85.7° Celsius). Scientists use these freezing and boiling points as the baseline, or standard, for measuring all temperatures.

At sea level, water freezes at 32° Fahrenheit (0° Celsius).

The water cycle

The water on Earth is continually recycled through a process called the water cycle. The water cycle takes water from the world's lakes and oceans and moves it from one place to another. Along the way, water is changed from a liquid to a gas and back to a liquid.

Evaporation and condensation

Water is continually recycled in the water cycle moving through four states, including evaporation, condensation, precipitation, and collection. Evaporation occurs when the sun's heat turns the water in lakes, rivers, streams, or oceans into water vapor or steam that rises into the air. As water vapor cools in the air, it **condenses** into liquid. **Gravity** acts on the collected water droplets, causing them to fall to Earth as rain or snow, which is also called precipitation. The precipitation that falls to Earth is absorbed in the ground and the water runs off into rivers, lakes, and oceans. The sun then heats the surface of these bodies of water, causing the water to evaporate and starting the water cycle all over again.

The sun evaporates water from lakes and oceans

Water vapor cools, condenses, and falls as rain or snow

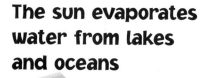

Water absorbed in the ground runs off into streams and lakes

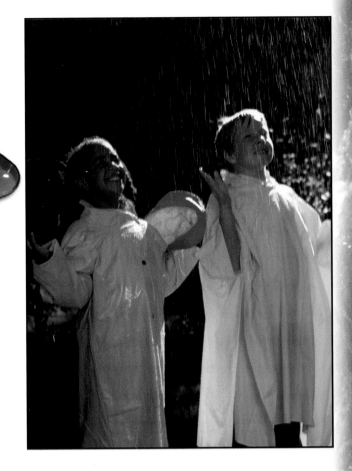

The first water on Earth

Scientists believe that all the water on Earth has been here since the planet was formed almost five billion years ago. At first, the Earth was a molten ball of **magma**. As it cooled, water vapor, and the chemical gases, carbon dioxide and nitrogen, were expelled from inside the Earth's core. This process is called degassing. When the Earth's temperature dropped below 212° Fahrenheit (100° Celsius), the gases condensed and formed clouds, which produced rain. Over thousands of years, the rain filled rivers, lakes, and oceans.

(above) Water falls as rain and either soaks into the Earth or evaporates into the air.

Photolysis

Billions of years ago, as the Earth cooled, it began to turn from a gassy orb into an orb with a molten core and a solid crust. Over time, the Earth cooled enough for the gases surrounding it in its **atmosphere** to condense. This triggered violent chemical and gas rains. Much of the gas escaped into space during a process called photolysis. Photolysis may have reduced the Earth's water **reserves** by 0.2 percent since the planet was formed.

(above) Billions of years ago, gassy storms helped form the Earth's watery atmosphere.

Water highways

Water is essential because it gives life. It also changes the way people live their lives. The Earth's oceans and lakes allowed explorers to visit lands never imagined before, which changed the world.

Thousands of years ago, when people first began to explore the Earth, they did not travel far from where they lived. Once they realized that waterways such as lakes, rivers, and oceans could take them to new places, they learned how to build boats and ships. These boats allowed explorers to make journeys for hunting, fishing, trading, politics, and moving to new places. Traveling by water let them go much farther than they could by land.

Early ocean adventurers

Ancient maps show the world as flat with monsters living at the edges. Early explorers thought they would sail right off of the Earth if they traveled too far. As explorers set out to seek new worlds, they proved that the Earth was round. Historians believe that people from South China made the first major ocean voyages about 4,000 years ago. Using simple boats, small groups sailed to Indonesia, New Guinea, and the Solomon Islands.

Portuguese explorer Ferdinand Magellan (standing in the small boat) was the first to sail around, or circumnavigate, the world in 1520. He died during the journey.

The Vikings

The Vikings were fearless sailors who crossed the Atlantic Ocean from Norway to Iceland around the year 815. In 982, Erik the Red sailed further west to Greenland. The Vikings were traders as well as explorers, so they built strong ships called longboats to hold their goods. In addition to crossing the Atlantic Ocean, the Vikings traveled in the Mediterranean Sea and in the Black Sea in Russia.

Ocean navigation

As early sailors learned more about **navigation**, they ventured further into the Pacific Ocean. They did not have compasses or maps to guide them, but used the stars, ocean currents, and animals, such as birds, to determine where land was.

Travel and trade

The Phoenicians were a group of ancient seafaring people who lived in the Middle East. They traded at seaports all around the Mediterranean Sea. Around 600 B.C., the Phoenicians sailed from the Red Sea to Africa. They traveled and **colonized**, or settled, in many areas along their routes.

The New World

European traders returning to Europe on land trade routes from Asia brought valuable goods such as spices and silks. Land journeys were long and dangerous, so traders wanted to find a way to get to Asia by sea. In 1492, Christopher Columbus convinced the king and queen of Spain to give him money to find a sea route to Asia. He sailed from Spain with three ships that year, and was the first European to arrive on the Bahamas Islands, in the Caribbean Sea. Columbus did not find the sea route he was looking for, but he did begin colonies and triggered a European race to claim North and South America.

Under the ground

Ground water is freshwater found beneath the surface of the Earth. The water collects in pores, cracks, and crevices and is the source of water for wells and springs.

Ground water

Ground water is rainwater or snowmelt that has soaked into the surface of the Earth. The water flows downward past dirt, sand, and gravel into the zone of aeration.

The zone of aeration is a porous area located above the water table. The water then flows through the water table into the zone of saturation, where the water pools in cracks and crevices. Pooled ground water often percolates, or seeps, underground into nearby streams, rivers, and lakes. Scientists estimate that 40 percent of the river water in the United States comes from ground water seepage.

Aquifers

The underground porous rock which ground water saturates, or soaks, are called aquifers. Aquifers vary in size. The Ogallala aquifer in the United States covers over 310,000 square miles (802,896 square km) from Nebraska to Texas. People draw water out of aquifers through wells or boreholes drilled into the Earth.

Springs

A spring is a small stream of water flowing naturally from the Earth. It bubbles up through the ground. Thermal springs, also called hot springs, occur in places where the water table is found at the Earth's surface. Ground water is heated deep within the Earth and rises to form pools of hot water. Many hot springs have a high mineral content.

Subterranean rivers

Subterranean, or underground, rivers form when volumes of ground water meet a layer of rock or clay that prevents it from going deeper. Pools of water form and as pressure builds, gravity pushes the water through cracks and openings in the rock. Underground water flows downward, wearing away rock and forming long tunnels that become underground rivers.

Lost desert city

Ubar was a famous trading city in the Arabian Desert almost 4,000 years ago. After it disappeared about 1,500 years ago, stories and legends said it had been destroyed by a fierce storm. In 1992, **archaeologists** found the city using photos taken from space. As they excavated, or dug, they discovered the ancient city was built around a water **reservoir** in a deep limestone cavern. Over the years, ground water dissolved the limestone and caves were formed. Eventually the ground became so thin that it could not bear the weight of the city's structures. The city collapsed, fell into the cavern, and was destroyed.

The ruins of the lost city of Ubar.

Surface water

Surface water is all the water found on the face of the Earth, including lakes and oceans. Surface water is easier to access than ground water because it can easily be seen.

Surface and ground

Surface water and ground water feed into each other. As ground water moves through the Earth, it eventually seeps into lakes or rivers. Surface water in lakes, rivers, and streams soaks back into the ground. This continuous process is called the water cycle.

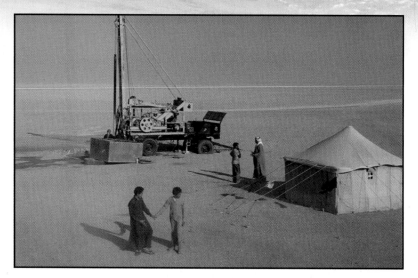

(above) Desert peoples drill for ground water in the Syrian Desert.

(below) A woman fills a water bucket from a pump near the Aral Sea in Munyak, Uzbekistan. Munyak was once a major freshwater fishing port until the sea began to shrink in the 1970s. The sea shrank because its water was used to irrigate cotton crops.

North America's Great Lakes, the world's largest freshwater system, as seen in a photo taken from space.

Seawater

The Earth's oceans cover 71 percent of the Earth's surface. On world maps, the oceans are divided, but they are all connected, with one flowing into the other. The Pacific Ocean, the largest ocean, covers 64,186,000 square miles (162,242,000 square km) and contains more than half of all the water in the world's oceans. The Pacific is nearly as big as the Atlantic and Indian Oceans combined. The Indian Ocean is about 12,467 feet (3,800 meters) deep. The smallest of the four, the Arctic Ocean, is mostly covered with ice. It is 3,662,445 square miles (9,485,000 square km).

Geysers

Geysers are hot springs that erupt and spew steaming hot water. The eruptions happen when ground water is heated to boiling temperature in a fracture, or crack, beneath the Earth's surface. As the water is heated, it turns to vapor and rises through the crack. About 300, or two thirds of the world's geysers are located in Yellowstone National Park in Wyoming, U.S.A. The most famous geyser is Old Faithful, which gets its name because it erupts every 76 minutes.

Old Faithful's steam is over 200° Fahrenheit (93° Celsius) and shoots over 180 feet (55 meters) into the air.

Shaping the Earth

Water in motion is a powerful force. In its different states, water can move and shape the Earth. Water and ice can even change the way a landscape looks by eroding solid rock.

Water erosion

Water **erosion** occurs when the force of moving water breaks off parts of rock or soil and carries them away. There are three main types of water erosion: sheet erosion, rill erosion, and mass erosion. Sheet erosion begins when a raindrop hits soil. Raindrops splash the soil particles, moving them short distances and loosening the surface. When rain falls faster than the soil can absorb it, the water collects and flows over the ground, carrying away the particles that were loosened by the raindrops.

Thousands of years of water erosion created these swirled sandstone rocks.

Rill erosion

Rill erosion is caused by water flowing in steady streams over the ground until it forms rills or channels. As the water moves through these rills, it picks up soil from the sides and bottoms, making the rills wider and deeper. Gullies are large rills formed when rushing water removes soil at the uphill end of a channel. Mass erosion, or slumping, occurs when a hillside becomes so heavy with water that large areas slide or creep downhill.

A man watches a beach house slide off of a beach and into the Gulf of Mexico after a storm.

Glaciers

About 10,000 years ago, during the last Ice Age, giant **glaciers** carved through the land, moving, scraping, and scarring the land. Today, glaciers are located on every continent except Australia. Most are found near the North and South Poles. Glaciers form when snow accumulates over many years and turns to ice. There are two types of glaciers. Valley glaciers flow down valleys. Continental glaciers move by extending outward in all directions from a central point.

How a glacier moves

A glacier moves by sliding on a thin layer of water underneath the ice. The water comes from glacial melting or from water that works its way through cracks in the glacial ice. When a glacier moves quickly, cracks called crevasses form on the surface. Glaciers carve out valleys by wearing away rocks and soil as they move. They scrape the underlying rock or pick up large pieces of rock and move them from one place to another. As glaciers shift, they push earth and rock forward, then leave debris behind when they begin to retreat. Glaciers retreat when more ice melts than accumulates. Raised temperatures, evaporation, and wind cause melting.

Glaciers usually retreat, or melt in the summer and move forward in the winter. This retreating glacier is in Glacier Bay, Alaska.

World of water

People's lifestyles are often determined by their access to water. Many communities develop near waterways that are sources of water for drinking, cleaning, and traveling from place to place. People living near water take advantage of the ready supply, but people in dry climates, such as deserts, spend much of their time searching for the water they need to live.

The need for water

All living things need water to survive. Today, due to modern methods of water **conservation** and **irrigation**, major cities thrive on desert sands. Los Angeles, a city where rain falls only two to three months a year, gets much of its water from Northern California and from the Colorado River in Nevada. Sometimes, people object to water in their area being rerouted to another location because it depletes their own water supply.

People adapt their lifestyles to meet water supplies. In rural areas where water is not piped into homes, people dig wells to tap into the local aquifer, or carry water from the nearest water body. They set out containers to collect rainwater and, in arctic regions, melt ice to get fresh water.

(right) Nomadic peoples, such as the Bedouin in the Arabian Desert, move from place to place, camping near oases where they find water.

Food supplies also depend on water. When water is plentiful, people grow a variety of food crops. In dry areas, much of the water must be used to irrigate crops.

Water ownership

There are no clear international laws for owning water. Disagreements arise over who has water and whether water is a **commodity** or a necessity of life. Battles and protests have been waged over the right to control water. The countries of Hungary and Slovakia have argued over control of the water in the Danube River. The Danube is the second largest river in Europe.

These people are protesting the lack of clean, affordable water in their homes.

Life in a rainforest

Rainforests, which cover about seven percent of the Earth's surface, are warm, densely vegetated environments where rain is almost always falling. Rainforests get about 80 inches (203 cm) of rain a year! They are home to millions of insects, reptiles, amphibians, birds, and mammals. Plants are large, green, and very lush. Indigenous, or native, peoples have lived in rainforests for hundreds of thousands of years.

These vines and lush plants grow in the rainforest.

21

Water and life

Water is a key part of the biosphere, the part of the Earth and the atmosphere where living things exist. All living things need freshwater. Without it, plants and animals dehydrate, or dry up, and die. Only three percent of the water on Earth is freshwater and plants, animals, and humans must share this resource.

Freshwater supply

Human beings need clean freshwater. Polluted water causes diseases in people who drink or wash with it. In some places, access to clean water is difficult and expensive. In most cities in North America, dirty and used water is taken away and cleaned through the sewage system. Outside of the cities, many people get their water through wells drilled into the ground. Access to water is as easy as turning on a tap. At the end of the month, the **public utility** sends a bill for the cost of pumping, piping, and cleaning the water used. It is not so easy to get clean water in many other parts of the world. For millions of people, there is no such thing as piped water in their houses. In Tegucigalpa, the capital city of Honduras in Central America, water is plentiful in wealthy neighborhoods, but not in poorer neighborhoods.

Raw, or untreated, sewage flows in the Ganges River in Varanasi, India. The Ganges is considered sacred to many Indians who swim in it and drink from it despite the pollution.

All residents of Tegucigalpa pay a fee to the city to have water piped in. The water flows everyday, all the time in wealthy neighborhoods. In poor neighborhoods, the water supply only runs once a month. People fill buckets and bottles with water so they will not run out before the water is turned on again. When they run out, poor people must buy water from companies that charge them a lot of money. Those who cannot afford to pay, drink **contaminated** water and many become ill.

Private water

Water is so essential to life that people do not like to say it is "owned." When the government in Bolivia, South America, **privatized** the water system of the city of Cochabamba, many people were upset. The company that ran the system raised water rates. The government passed a law that prevented people from taking water from rivers or even rainbarrels. The people of Cochabamba protested and after violent fights the water system was returned to the people.

Water and life

The human body is about 70 percent water. The brain is also 70 percent water. Blood is 82 percent water and the lungs are nearly 80 percent water. Water dissolves the nutrients and minerals taken in with food. Chemical reactions turn the nutrients into fuel that enables humans to grow and help the body repair itself. Water molecules carry substances to organs, muscles, and bones. It also carries away the waste products that are no longer needed. If an organism does not get enough water, it dehydrates because there is not enough water in the body to perform all these tasks.

Egyptian women carry drinking water on their heads as they walk in the Nile River.

Uses of water

Water is used by people in everyday life. Water is also used in industry to make things and in farming to grow plants and water livestock. The use of water involves everyone because everyone is a consumer. Conserving water benefits everyone.

Irrigation in farming

One of the greatest uses of water is on farms. All plants need water, but in dry, arid areas where rain is scarce, farmers must use irrigation to water their crops. Irrigation has been used for thousands of years in countries such as China, Egypt, and India. In the Southwestern United States, irrigation was practiced by Native Americans, and later by the Spanish who settled in California in the 1500s.

Today's methods

Today, California farms grow vegetables and fruits for markets all over the world. Farms use sprinklers and **drip irrigation** systems to water crops. Water is taken from ground water, rivers, and reservoirs. California farms use a network of 100 computerized weather stations to help them irrigate. The network tells farmers how much moisture is in the soil so that they can decide when to irrigate and how much water to use.

Farm workers clear out furrows of irrigation water between rows of crops in Sudan. Several methods are used to irrigate cropland. In free-flooding, large areas of land are flooded with water from canals and ditches. Check-flooding takes place when water flows over strips of land between levees or ridges. Other ways to irrigate are with pipes, sprinklers, and drip hoses.

Water conservation

The California irrigation management system helps conserve water. Irrigation is needed to grow crops, but irrigation can also be a hazard to farming. Sometimes, ground water aquifers, or supplies of water dry up and there is no more water to use. Water can also erode soil, removing the nutrients that help plants grow strong and healthy.

Water in industry

Large quantities of water are used in factories that make products such as detergents for cleaning, and in car and appliance manufacturing. Factories use water to cool machines and tools, and as a solvent to dissolve chemicals.

Water in mining

Water is also used in the mining industry, and in drilling for oil. In mining, water is used to separate **ore** from rocks, to cool drills, and to remove unwanted materials from the ore after **processing**. In oil drilling, water is often pumped into wells under pressure to force oil up to the Earth's surface.

Commercialization of water

Some companies are drawing great amounts of water from aquifers to produce bottled water. This means that water, which is normally free for public use, is turned into a commodity that people buy. Water bottling plants create jobs, but some people think the bottlers take too much water from springs. In Michigan, residents sued the Nestle Company to prevent the company from taking 400 gallons (1515 liters) of spring water per minute from a local stream. The judge ordered Nestle Company to stop taking from the stream, but allowed the company to take 175 gallons (662 liters) of ground water per minute only eleven miles (18 km) away.

A gold mine worker operates a machine that separates ore from rock using a water slurry, or mixture.

Treating water

Thousands of years ago, the ancient Romans built aqueducts to transport clean water from the Roman countryside into the city. The ancient Roman sewage system took polluted water away from the city in much the same way that modern sewage systems do.

From sewage to clean water

Even when the water in lakes and rivers looks clean, it may still be unfit for drinking. Household water is cleaned in water treatment plants where dirt, **bacteria**, parasites, and chemical impurities are removed.

At the plant

Cleaning the water is a three-stage process at a sewage treatment plant. The first step involves removing large objects or solids from the water. Solids that settle out of the water are put into drying lagoons or pools. Next, the sludge, or mud, that settles to the bottom, and the wastewater are treated with chemicals. A chemical that acts like bleach is put into the water to kill germs. The cleaned water is then returned to rivers and lakes and the remaining sludge is put into tanks where it is broken down by bacteria. The leftovers are used to make fertilizer or burned in an **incinerator**.

Graywater

Graywater is untreated household wastewater from kitchen sinks, or laundry water that has not come in contact with toilet waste.

Workers at a sewage treatment plant adjust water levels at the plant's graywater tanks.

Re-use

Graywater can be reused for other purposes, such as landscape irrigation. Using graywater saves freshwater for drinking, cooking, and bathing. Graywater is good for the soil but should not be used on edible plants, such as vegetables. Graywater lowers freshwater use, relieves the strain on treatment facilities, conserves energy, and reclaims nutrients that would otherwise be wasted. Graywater is often used to water large green areas such as golf courses and public parks.

In the old days

For thousands of years, cities did not have sewers. Wastewater was dumped into the streets and pedestrians walked on steppingstones to avoid the muck. The waste eventually drained into the local water source where it polluted drinking water. The polluted water caused diseases such as cholera and diarrhea. Cholera killed many people before scientists discovered that contaminated water was its cause. Today, modern sewage treatment kills disease-causing bacteria in sewage.

Tanks full of churning sewage at the National Park Service sewage treatment plant at Old Faithful. Last year, visitors and employees in Yellowstone National Park produced roughly 90 gallons (341 liters) of sewage per person. At the same time, most visitors expect the park to be pristine, as if untouched by humans.

Water power

Water that flows from rivers and waterfalls is an important power source. For hundreds of years, people have used the power and force of water to run mills that grind grain, and cut wood and shingles. Today, water's power has been harnessed to create electric energy for light and power.

Electric energy

Electricity exists in nature as static electricity that produces lightning in a storm, or gives you a sudden spark in the winter when you touch metal. Until the 1800s, no one knew how to make or use electricity. For hundreds of years, people heated their homes and cooked food by burning coal or wood in fireplaces or stoves. They used **kerosene** lamps and candles for light and cooled food with ice.

The Itaipu dam hydroelectric power plant in Paraguay and Brazil took sixteen years to build.

The need for electricty

In the late 1800s, several inventions were made that required electricity to run. One invention was the lightbulb, and many more inventions requiring electricty have followed. Electricity can be created in a number of ways. One early way was through machines that converted steam power into electric power.

Hydroelectric power

Another way to create electricity is by harnessing the power of falling water. Hydro comes from the Greek word for water. Hydroelectric power plants convert the kinetic, or moving energy, in falling water into electricity. Where no natural waterfalls exist, rivers are dammed and water is forced over embankments.

Steam rises from a pipeline at a geothermal power plant in Nesjavellir, Iceland. Geothermal power plants harness hot steam from magma deep in the Earth to create electricity to power or heat. This plant sends heated water to the nearby city of Reykjavik.

Renewable energy

Hydroelectric power is currently the world's largest renewable energy source. Electricity is generated in power plants by water flowing through enormous engines called turbines. A turbine is a spear-shaped shaft with a series of blades mounted on it. The turbine is connected to a generator that converts energy from the turbine into electrical energy.

Wheels of water

Water wheels have been used since ancient times to convert falling water into power. Water flows over the wheel, causing a set of mounted paddles to turn. Water wheels were located near waterfalls to capture the weight and force of falling water. The most common use of water wheels was to power mills. Hundreds of years ago, mills were used to cut timber and grind grain into flour. Timber mills were called sawmills, and grain mills were called gristmills. Some mills even combed sheep's wool. Those mills were called carding mills. When electricity became widely used, water mills became less efficient and most closed forever.

Water fight

People go to great efforts to control the supply of fresh water. Water is a resource that requires careful use and management by the people who use it, governments, and industries.

Pollution control

Water pollution is a serious problem in many countries. The three main sources of pollution are industrial waste, sewage from cities and towns, and agricultural chemicals used to protect crops from pests and disease. Industrial waste is the chemical leftovers, or byproducts, from manufacturing. Sometimes, companies knowingly or unknowingly dump this untreated waste into nearby waterways. The chemicals poison and kill plants and animals. Untreated sewage from cities and towns sometimes leaks out into lakes and streams from treatment plants. The sewage contaminates the water and gives swimmers ear and eye infections. Agricultural chemicals can **leach** into ground water supplies and poison drinking water. Many countries have laws to control water pollution, but it is difficult to make certain everyone obeys the law.

How we use water

In many parts of North America, water is often so plentiful that people never think about how they use it. They take long showers, water their lawns, and let their faucets run without monitoring their use. It may seem like there is a limitless supply of freshwater, but overuse of water can deplete aquifers or lower artificial lakes, or reservoirs.

Dead fish from a toxic chemical spill litter the edge of a stream.

Villagers in India's Narmada Valley have been fighting to stop the building of dams on the Narmada River for many years. The 30 major dams and 3,000 smaller dams on the river will force about 200,000 people out of their homes and villages forever. These women are willing to risk their lives to protest a dam that is flooding their homes.

Dams and reservoirs

About 4,500 years ago, the ancient Egyptians built a dam to capture water and store it in a reservoir so they would have fresh water for drinking. The main reasons for damming rivers today are to provide hydroelectric power and to control flooding. A reservoir needs to be emptied during the rainy season so it can store water for the dry season. If it is too full, it may overflow, and cause the walls to collapse and the water to flood surrounding areas. Building a dam alters a river valley, often flooding the area. People are forced to move when their homes are flooded by dam building.

Three Gorges Dam

About 400 million people live along the banks of the Yangtze River in China, the third longest river in the world. The Yangtze has flooded many times, destroying homes and crops, and killing thousands of people. In 1997, the Chinese government began a project to build a dam across the Three Gorges section of the river. When finished, it will require the flooding of thousands of villages, and hundreds of towns and cities. Over one million people will be displaced. The Chinese government says the dam is necessary to control the level of the river and to prevent flooding. It will also become a major source of electrical power, producing 18,000 megawatts of electricity.

A ship sails through one of the ship locks of the massive Three Gorges Dam.

Glossary

archaeologist A person who studies cultures of the past

atmosphere The layer of gases that surround Earth

bacteria Tiny one-celled organisms

chemical A substance produced by chemistry

colonize When a group of people settle in a land but remain citizens of their native country

commodity Something that is bought and sold

condense To turn from a gas to a liquid

conservation Using carefully, so as not to waste

consumer Someone who buys and uses goods and services

contaminate To make impure or unclean

drip irrigation A type of irrigation whereby water is dripped onto soil very slowly

element A substance that cannot be broken down into smaller parts by chemical means

erosion To wear away over time

glacier A slowly moving mass of ice

gravity A natural force that pulls objects toward the center of the Earth

incinerator A furnace used for burning waste materials

irrigation Supplying water to land by use of ditches, pipes, and canals

kerosene A flammable oil used as fuel

leach To slowly drain through something

magma Hot melted rock formed within the Earth

mineral A natural, non-living substance made up of one or more elements

molecule The smallest particle of matter, consisting of one or more atoms

navigation Charting the course for a ship or aircraft

ore A rock or mineral containing useful metal

privatize To change the ownership or control of an industry from public to private

processing Preparing for final use

public utility A company that provides a public service, such as water, gas, and electricity

reserves Things set aside for later use

reservoir An artificial lake used to collect and store water

solar system The nine planets and other bodies that orbit the sun

solvent A substance that dissolves or disperses another substance

transparent Something that is clear, or see through

Index

1 2 3 4 5 6 7 8 9 0 Printed in the U.S.A. 3 2 1 0 9 8 7 6 5 4